台所 • Las Cocinas • Küchen
Cucine • מטבח • Cozinhas • Kitch
nes • 廚房 • Mutfaklar • 부엌들 • Le Cucine
chen • Keukens • ห้องครัวหลายห้อง • Les cuis
Cozinhas • Kitchens • 台所 • Las Cocinas • I
房 • Mutfaklar • 부엌들 • Le Cucine • מטבח
ns • ห้องครัวหลายห้อง • Les cuisines • 廚房 •
ens • 台所 • Las Cocinas • Küchen • Keukens
ucine • מטבח • Cozinhas • Kitchens • 台所 • L
sines • 廚房 • Mutfaklar • 부엌들 • Le Cucine
hen • Keukens • ห้องครัวหลายห้อง • Les cuisi
nhas • Kitchens • 台所 • Las Cocinas • Küche
ar • 부엌들 • Le Cucine • מטבח • Cozinhas •
รัวหลายห้อง • Les cuisines • 廚房 • Mutfaklar
Las Cocinas • Küchen • Keukens • ห้องครัว

Colors for Living

KITCHENS

BY JILL PILAROSCIA WITH SANDRA RAGAN

First published in the United States of America by:
Rockport Publishers, Inc.
146 Granite Street
Rockport, Massachusetts 01966
Telephone: (508) 546-9590
Fax: (508) 546-7141

First Thailand edition 1995,
published by Rockport Publishers, Inc. for:
Page One (Thailand) Ltd
230 Soi Thonglor 8
Sukhumvit 55
Bangkok 10110
Thailand
Telephone/Fax: (662) 391-3657

First Singapore edition 1995,
published by Rockport Publishers, Inc. for:
Page One
The Bookshop Pte Ltd
Blk 4, Pasir Panjang Road
#08-33 Alexandra Distripark
Singapore 0512
Telephone: (65) 2730128
Fax: (65) 2730042

ISBN 1-56496-102-8

10 9 8 7 6 5 4 3 2 1

Art Director: Laura Herrmann
Designer: Nick Clark
Layout and Production: KBB Design
Cover Photograph: Rick Chapman

Printed in Hong Kong

KITCHENS

ROCKPORT
PUBLISHERS

Rockport Publishers, Inc.
Rockport, Massachusetts

COLORS FOR LIVING...

Colors For Life

Photo: Tim Street-Porter

At one time or another each of us has marveled at the way a colorful sunrise can lift our spirits, or a magnificent red sunset can complete the day.

Creating living spaces with these same alluring colors can inspire each of us. For me, this new series of books is a recognition of something I had come to expect and had long taken for granted ... color in my life.

I'm sure it will be the same for you!

— *Sandra Ragan*

ACKNOWLEDGMENTS

I would like to express gratitude to all the designers, architects, and photographers who have graciously contributed images for this book. I would like to thank Emily Keenan for her invaluable assistance on all aspects of the project. Thanks also to Sandra Ragan for editorial guidance, and to Brenda Edgar for photo research assistance. I must acknowledge the support of my husband Jack, my two children, Blake and Emerald, and finally, two mentors and friends in the world of color, Beverly Thome and Laura Guido-Clark.

TABLE OF CONTENTS

Photo: Tim Street-Porter

Photo: Agnes Bourne, Inc.

PREFACE

My color pathway was revealed to me when I was only two years old. My father grew dahlias of all varieties in the side yard, and I can still remember toddling through row upon row of vividly colored red, yellow, and pink flowers. Recently my parents sent me some baby pictures, and, to my surprise and delight, I found among them a photograph of me in that very garden. The brilliant colors of the flowers in the picture confirmed beyond a doubt the accuracy of my early color memory.

The rest of my color story follows a natural progression. During a slide presentation at the San Francisco Art Institute, the instructor began to discuss the "Color Field" painters Frank Stella, Morris Louis, and Mark Rothko. I realized then that communication could occur through the sole medium of color. You did not even have to paint a realistic image to illustrate your point—color could speak on its own!

After graduation I found an ad in the newspaper that read: *Help wanted, person to paint large fields of color.* I took a position as a housepainter on the all-male painting crew of Local Color and began painting multicolored Victorian homes. I reasoned that painting on a building could not be much different from painting on a canvas. Within four weeks I became the company's color consultant, and I began creating custom color schemes for discriminating homeowners.

From my job selecting colors for the exterior of buildings, it was natural to start creating interior color palettes. Project scopes and scales just keep evolving. Color work is a great teacher and great inspiration. I have seen clients hate certain hues. I often ask them about their associations with that hue. Sometimes we discover that the qualities of the color they dislike represent something that's missing in their lives. If possible, I then try to incorporate small doses of that color into their environment.

I have observed myself going through color phases, favoring a particular hue. For example, I may become fascinated with green and explore every nuance of the hue: light, dark, blue-green, yellow-green. I will find this color turning up in many of my color schemes, because I find it inspires me personally. It is my wish that this book be an inspiration to others seeking their own personal color pathway.

— Jill Pilaroscia

INTRODUCTION

We delight in the colors of the world around us: the evening sunset, a rainbow, a spring meadow in bloom. Inside, the color of a room creates atmosphere; in the kitchen it sets the mood, arouses the senses, and can make good food look even better. Color acts as a seventh sense. Like the other senses, color can communicate loudness, softness, distance, and other important information about the surrounding area. Just as a room's furnishings tell us where we are in the house, its color tells us how we should feel about it.

Do you remember asking your childhood friends, "What is your favorite color?" Even as very young children, we respond strongly to color stimuli. Perhaps you hoped that both you and your childhood friend favored the same hue. You may even have formed an opinion of someone based on their color preferences. Subjective response is often based on color memories. As a child, breakfast at my grandmother's farm always consisted of poached eggs freshly gathered from the farmyard. The golden color of the yolk would spread across my blue-and-white-patterned plate. These colors still vividly recall to me the flavors and atmosphere of that early experience.

Think of the ways color provides us with information in our daily lives. If your were without your watch, you could approximate the time of day by observing sky colors. We are able to drive safely by recognizing the color signals for stop, go, and yield. Walking the aisles of the grocery store you select products bottled in blue to wash your clothes and green to freshen your air. We have learned color associations which are used by marketing professionals to influence our purchases.

Color gives interiors vitality. Kitchen color trends have traveled the spectrum—from all white to the mod colors popular in the sixties. Trends or not, many people continue to regard neutral-color spaces as safe and familiar, relying on accessories —such as a pillow or a rug—to brighten up a bland room. It seems that the more color moves from "functional" to purely decorative purposes, the less confident people are about using it. Color choice becomes a ground we can be judged on. In fact, color has always been a vehicle of expression in our culture and our art. By becoming more sensitive to the color around us, we, like artists, can have the courage to bring the vitality of color back into our homes and our lives.

Take a moment to reflect upon your favorite colors. What memories come to mind? See if these thoughts can help you set a direction to develop a color palette for your kitchen.

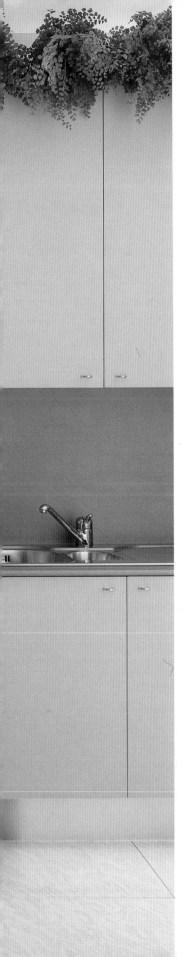

HISTORY OF THE KITCHEN

The evolution of the modern kitchen began when primitive people started to cook food and brought a source of fire into their shelters. For centuries cooking was done over an open flame; kitchens were hot and dangerous. Smoke-blackened walls and bare stone floors made up the unfriendly decor. Except for local building materials, such as red and yellow clays, color was not a concern—function was.

In the 1700s, coal became the fuel of choice and the design of the hearth changed. Trade routes to the Far East opened, bringing exotic new spices and vibrantly colored mineral pigments with them. As kitchens became less smoke-filled and more colorful, "dining" rooms in or near the kitchen took shape.

During the Victorian era, large blocks of ice served as refrigerator-freezers, stoves did double duty as heaters, and cooktop burners came into use. As travel became easier, more Europeans and Americans toured the ancient sites of Rome, Greece, and Egypt. The brilliant colors of the Mediterranean inspired travelers, and rich greens, purples, blues, and reds made their way from the ancient world to the Victorian kitchen.

In the 1930s and 1940s, large wartime inventions, such as airplanes, helped small kitchen inventions, such as appliances, take off. Machine-age kitchens had chrome accents and cool blue, green, and gray palettes. The introduction of titanium dioxide to paint made whites look brighter, and modern kitchens followed their lead—becoming bright, white, and uncluttered.

The 1950s marked a turning point in kitchen design. Plastic laminates, linoleum, and other new materials offered hygienic, easy-to-clean surfaces. Stylish kitchen-layouts were streamlined and efficient. As American paint companies launched hundreds of new colors for interiors, kitchens bloomed in pink, orange, violet, and anything-goes palettes. The age of avocado and harvest gold appliances had begun.

CURRENT TRENDS

Today, the kitchen is the heart of the home. Hectic lifestyles and two-career families are now the norm, not the exception. Time for socializing and relaxing with friends and family has become scarce. Thankfully, eating remains one of life's necessities and pleasures, and cooking meals still brings people together. Children do homework while dinner is being prepared, and guests join their hosts chopping vegetables or pouring wine. The modern kitchen provides nourishment for both body and soul. No longer bound by rigid traditions, today's kitchen has evolved from a hot smoky shed set away from the house to a stylish haven whose colors, finishes, and building materials are limited only by the imagination.

The myriad of styles and colors available for your kitchen can be difficult to choose from. Knowing the popular trends in color, or even being ahead of the next color cycle, can be invaluable in the difficult process of selecting the right colors.

Today, the movement toward "green" products, recycled materials, renewable resources, and energy conservation is strongly influencing color trends. "Earth" colors are showing up everywhere, from neutrals like linen colors, cool grays, and warm muted browns to yellows, deep greens with black undertones, and rich reddish purples. Mandarin orange, gray-greens, and silver-greens are also becoming popular, along with very earthy reds. To offset all of these deep tones, think of colors in the brilliant blue and parrot green family.

Regardless of what you choose, remember: there are no *wrong* colors, only wrong color combinations. Color choices based on personal taste rather than on trends will always survive the test of time.

PLANNING YOUR KITCHEN

Before building a new kitchen, remodeling an existing one, or simply sprucing things up with a new coat of paint, it helps to be familiar with the properties of color: understanding how colors work together and how they influence one another gives you the foundation to build the environment you want.

COLOR WHEEL

The color wheel is the most useful tool to help you understand the relationships of color—one to another, and of groups of colors together. Use the wheel as you explore color for your kitchen.

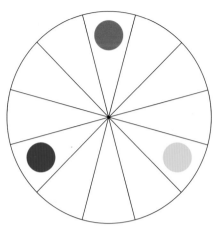

PRIMARY COLORS

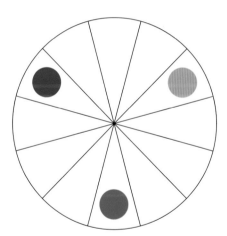

SECONDARY COLORS

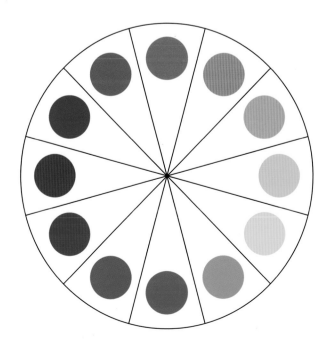

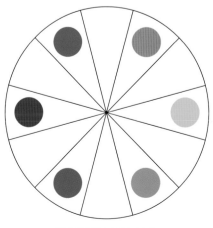

TERTIARY COLORS

COLOR THEORY

Hue is the formal term for color, or color name, such as red, yellow, or blue. *Value* is the relative lightness or darkness of a color. Colors with white added are *tints* and colors with black added are known as *shades*. *Saturation* is the intensity or brightness of a color, and *temperature* is the perceived warmth or coolness of a color.

Warm colors—red, orange, and yellow—are all associated with sunshine and fire. They are located on the left side of the color wheel. Inviting, friendly and extroverted colors, they advance visually and can make a large kitchen appear smaller. These colors can generate a quality of light, like sunshine, and brighten a dark room. Saturated warm colors are invigorating, yet not everyone can tolerate the stimulus in their environment. Pastel tints of peach, rose, and yellow are more popular for large areas in the kitchen.

Cool colors—green, blue-green, and blue—are associated with the sky, water, and the woods. They are located on the right side of the color wheel. A small kitchen will appear larger when these calming, restful and introverted colors, which recede visually, are used. Pastel cool tones may create an icy atmosphere, so kitchens with abundant natural light accommodate the cool tones best. Very light cool colors can feel cold and bleak, while more saturated cool colors feel mysterious and soothing.

Colors are combined to form various *chords*, or schemes. *Monochromatic* color schemes use only one color, or variation on a theme, such as white, black, and gray in combination. *Analogous* color schemes use three colors next to each other on the color wheel (or their tints and shades), such as red, red-orange, and yellow, or red-orange, yellow, and pink (which is a tint of red). *Complementary* color schemes employ colors from opposite sides of the color wheel, for example, purple and yellow.

A *split complement* scheme using the same example would pair the two colors next to yellow on the color wheel—yellow-orange or yellow-green—with purple. A *triad* color scheme uses three colors, or their shades or tints, that are spaced fairly equally around the color wheel, for example, red, yellow, and blue.

● BASIC COLOR CHORDS

Monochromatic

Analogous

Split Complementary

Triad

COLOR BASICS

How do you envision your kitchen? Color plays a major role in how you feel about your environment. Begin to design your kitchen by listing adjectives that define the kitchen you want to call your own.

— *Happy, Bright, Cheerful*

— *Natural, Airy, Open*

— *Sleek, Sophisticated, Stark*

— *Simple, Clean, Restful*

If you selected "cheerful, airy, and simple," you could match them with the colors yellow, white, and red. If you selected "restful and open," you might use the colors blue and green. This simple process can help you establish your color direction.

Along with the color direction, consider the other factors that influence the project:

— *What elements currently exist that will not be changed?* Then explore the new avenues open in color, texture, and materials.

— *What specific materials or finishes do you have in mind?*

— *Are they in color?*

— *Which color families are you most comfortable with in your kitchen?*

— *Which color or colors do you wish to avoid?*

Color affects interior space. The location of color stimuli within an interior space influences a room's character, atmosphere, and how people will react to it. A color suitable for the floor changes when you apply it to the ceiling.

To successfully plan your color scheme you must decide on the degree of vitality or mood you want the room to have, for example, bright, cheerful, restful, etc. Once you settle on an overall "mood" for your kitchen, general principles of color combining should be followed. You may think of choosing your

Photo: Alan Weintraub
Design: Noble/Simon

kitchen colors in much the same way an artist thinks of choosing the palette for a painting.

Collect samples of the materials you are considering, then study the interrelationship between your colors, materials, and finishes. Be sure to have a variety of textures, such as gloss, matte, and satin.

Three steps in tonal value between colors are all it takes for the eye to see color differences. Variety in tonal value helps to articulate a room. A dark-value floor, medium-value walls and cabinets, and a light ceiling all define a room.

Using the chart on page 21, learn how colors are perceived on different surfaces in the kitchen. For example, would you want a red ceiling if you had a small space? It would make you feel closed in because red would move toward you, bringing the ceiling down upon your spirit. Every color choice you make should be studied in terms of the effect it will have on you and your environment.

A KITCHEN INVENTORY CHECKLIST

It is a good idea to get an overview of the color decisions you may need to make for the design of your kitchen. By being aware of these items, you can take the proactive rather than the reactive approach to color selections. You should consider color for the largest surface areas first: floor, cabinets, walls, and counters. Then consider your choice for smaller areas. As areas grow smaller in size, the chromatic intensity may be increased proportionately.

— *DOMINANT AREAS: cabinetry, walls, floor and ceiling*
— *SUBDOMINANT AREAS: counter, backsplash*
— *SMALL AREAS: appliances, fixtures*
— *ACCESSORIES: hardware, lighting fixtures, textiles*

Fill in your color idea after each item you may be considering for the room. You may wish to develop several schemes, so fill in an inventory sheet for each. This is an excellent process to help sharpen your ideas. If you have your heart set on a black counter, brainstorm on what materials come in black. Stone, ceramic, plastic laminate: which one matches your budget or style?

APPLIANCES
sinks
stove, cooktop and hood
oven and microwave
dishwasher
refrigerator
trash compactor
small appliances:
food processor, coffee
maker, juicer, etc.

FLOOR FINISHES
ceramic tile
stone
wood
vinyl tile
sheet vinyl
concrete

FURNITURE
tables
chairs
sideboards

CABINETRY
wood or painted finish
plastic laminate
glass front doors
open shelving
freestanding island

WALL AND CEILING FINISHES
eggshell or high-gloss paint
wallcovering
stenciling
faux finishes or *trompe l'oeil*

HARDWARE AND LIGHT FIXTURES
chrome
brass
iron
porcelain
outlet/switch plate covers

COUNTERTOP AND BACKSPLASH
tile
stone
plastic laminate
solid surfacing material
metal/laminates
butcher block
concrete
stainless steel
copper

ACCESSORIES
pot racks
linens
collections
wine racks

INTERIOR FUNDAMENTALS

Today the color choices for the kitchen are limitless. Appliances and fixtures come in virtually any color. The down side of kitchen design is cost: because so many permanent fixtures and appliances are integral to kitchen design, this room can cost more per square foot than any room in the house. Careful planning is a must. An attitude of inquiry will help you get started planning the space.

Photo: David Livingston

— *How does your kitchen work with the rest of the house?*

Colors in adjoining rooms that are visible from the kitchen should be considered in your design choices.

— *How visible do you want your kitchen to be from other rooms?*

If you want to increase its visibility, choose bright or contrasting colors which will draw attention to the kitchen.

— *Do you have a design style in your house you'd like to match?*

If you have a traditional living room and dining room that adjoin the kitchen the best color scheme will be one that enhances this style.

— *How will you use your kitchen for entertaining, family, or special needs?*

When you understand its language, color can help create the kind of feeling you want.

— *Are there pieces of equipment that you want to use as you renovate or redecorate?*

If you have a stove in blue or a green refrigerator, consider whether you want to highlight or hide them when selecting your kitchen color palette.

— *Are you considering changing the lighting in your kitchen?*

Lighting does affect the color you select so pick your colors under the same type of lighting you will be using. Natural light from the north is cold and has a greenish cast. South light is warm and pink. East light is harsh, has a yellowish cast, and tends to bleach out the appearance of colors, while west light is radiant red-orange. Fluorescent lights give off a blue tint unless color-corrected tubes are used. Tungsten and halogen are very bright and give off a yellow and blue cast, respectively. Incandescent lights bathe colors in a yellow-orange glow. It pays to be aware of lighting.

— *What is your budget?*

COLOR IN THE KITCHEN

Color Effects in the Interior Space

The location (top, sides, bottom) of color stimulus within the interior space can make a great deal of difference in a room's character, the way it is perceived psychologically, and the subsequent reactions to it. A particular hue that is perfectly suitable on the floor may elicit an entirely different reaction when applied to the ceiling.

COLOR	CEILING	WALLS	FLOOR
Red	Heavy	Advancing	Alert
Pink	Delicate	Aggression-Inhibiting	Unfamiliar
Orange	Stimulating	Luminous	Activating
Yellow	Luminous	Exciting	Diverting
Green	Protective	Calm	Relaxing
Blue	Celestial	Cool	Substantial
*Purple	Unexpected	Regal	Exclusive
Brown	Oppressive	Secure	Stable
Gray	Shadowy	Neutral	Neutral
White	Light	Sterile	Touch-Inhibiting
Black	Oppressive	Ominous	Abstract

Reprinted with permission of Van Nostrand Reinhold Company, from *Color and Light in Man-Made Environments*, by Frank H. Mahnke and Rudolph H. Mahnke. Copyright 1978 by Van Nostrand Reinhold company.

*Purple has been added by the author to Mahnke's original list.

BRAVE NEW COLORS
Strong and Energetic Primary Color Schemes

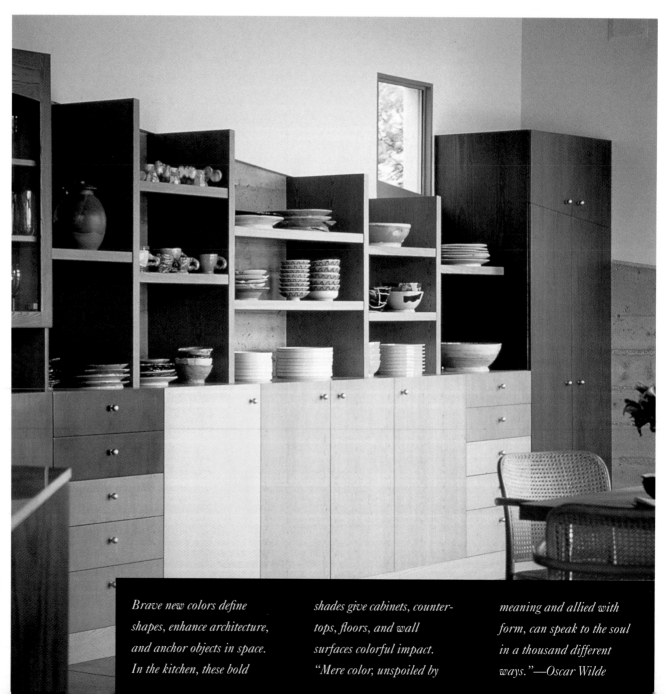

Photo: Tim Street-Porter

Brave new colors define shapes, enhance architecture, and anchor objects in space. In the kitchen, these bold shades give cabinets, countertops, floors, and wall surfaces colorful impact. "Mere color, unspoiled by meaning and allied with form, can speak to the soul in a thousand different ways."—Oscar Wilde

In the geography of the modern home, the status of the kitchen has been elevated to new heights. Now a central command post for the family's daily activities, as well as an eating place and a place for entertaining, the kitchen's white, utilitarian finishes have given way to brave new colors. Attention-grabbing red, yellow, and blue primaries, and strong secondary shades of orange, purple, and green add up to dynamic design in the kitchen.

Colors that once would have been found only in the parlor or formal dining room are turning up in even bolder shades on modern kitchen's walls, cabinets, and countertops.

Brave new colors stimulate the appetite and activate the senses; their bold hues will energize you each time you step into your kitchen.

Unusual shape— not color—creates the real drama in this kitchen, but yellow tones in the wood floor show the island's green form to advantage.

● **BRAVE NEW COLORS PALETTE**

Combinations of warm colors, such as Chanel red, daffodil yellow, and mandarin orange, create a lively, cheerful atmosphere in the kitchen. Cooler analogous colors, such as ivy green and riviera blue, are vivid together, but make their surroundings more tranquil.

 Riviera Blue

 Chanel Red

 Ivy Green

 Daffodil Yellow

 Mandarin Orange

 Iris Purple

Photo: Kitchen by Piero Lissoni, Boffi, Milan, Italy

Photo: Alan Weintraub

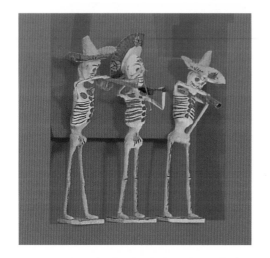

Cornsilk Yellow

Red Ember

Sunset Orange

Strong red on the fireplace marries function and color symbolism. Daffodil, orange, and teal colors on a dining set further develop the strong color palette.

Topaz

Gray Sand

Pompeii Red

A spicy curry of yellows, oranges and reds warm this small kitchen and make an ideal environment for cooking. Exaggerated drawer pulls and a stainless steel sink reflect light and add character to the room.

Photo: David Hale

Red Geranium

Cobalt

Wheat

Though this large kitchen easily accommodates a full-size totem pole, brave, saturated red walls bring the room a more comfortable scale.

Photo: Steve Vierra

Photo: Steve Vierra

Photo: Tim Street-Porter

Daffodil Yellow

Riviera Blue

True Red

Chromatic fireworks in primary yellow, blue, and red ignite this rustic kitchen. Bright yellow tiles and furnishings move the eye upward and heighten the impact of the blue-glazed countertop and lower wall.

Chrome Yellow

Carnelian

Vineyard Green

In this arched, open kitchen, saturated chrome yellow walls focus attention inward. Floor tiles in earthy golden hues have a calming influence on their surroundings.

Photo: Tim Street-Porter

Herb Green

Cornhusk Yellow

Lilac

Photo: Tim Street-Porter

Cabinets polychromed in eight different colors break up the lines of this kitchen. Glass insets, and stripes and fragments of color make ordinary built-ins dynamic.

Photo: Kitchen in "Merano" finish by Allmilmo

Bright Red

Spinach Green

Canary Yellow

Opposing colors emphasize each other in this kitchen's rainbow of storage drawers. White tile on the floor and backsplash focuses attention on the accents.

Sage Green

Golden Glow

Ochre

A wall of ochre-patterned tile gives depth to this understated color scheme of green and yellow.

Photo: Alan Weintraub

Garnet

Fern Green

Oriental Blue

A wall painted daffodil yellow heats up strong shades of analogous blue and green. The rectangular rhythm of the doors and windows repeats in the shape of sun-scorched red tile on the countertop. In this kitchen, color defines shape, and produces a tonic and vigorous atmosphere.

Photo: Kitchen by ALNO

Shell Coral

Gray Dawn

Bold, hard-edged color defines the elements of a kitchen: counter-top, cabinets, and floor. Black gives the soft orange tones in the woodwork graphic strength.

Citrus Yellow

Celery Green

Olive Gray

Photo: Tim Street-Porter

Light gives this kitchen its fresh, lively appeal; glossy yellow and white finishes shine alongside polished metal counters, hardware, and molding.

Photo: "Optima Gravel" finish kitchen by Allmilmo Corporation

Grenadine Orange

Fawn

Shadow Blue

Brave new colors in geometric shapes add dimension to the neutral tones of this kitchen/dining area. A vivid orange stripe advances in the room: highlighting a single row of cabinets while the others fade into the background.

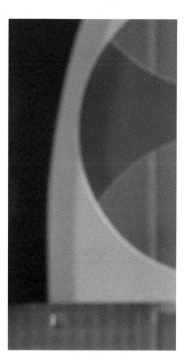

 Blue Lake

 Rouge

 Kumquat Orange

Jewel tones of red, yellow, and blue set the stage for this Moorish-inspired kitchen design. Shape and color draw the eye upward on chairs pierced with trefoils and arches.

Photo: Alan Weintraub

ECLECTIC CONTRASTS
Crisp, Sophisticated Shades

Against these crisp, sophisticated palettes, colorful foods, whether set out for presentation or preparation, take center stage. "Colors are actors, they constitute a cast; they perform."
—George Rickey

Photo: Rick Chapman

Monochromatic kitchen color schemes based on black, white, and gray, and accented with small proportions of color, act as a clean, crisp backdrop for cooking, conversing, or just relaxing.

Contrasts in hue and in value are visually arousing; our attention is constantly drawn to the places where edges meet. Contrast and comparison help us evaluate a color image. The greater the contrast in value—black against white—the stronger the visual message. When color is introduced into this palette, its impact is heightened.

● ECLECTIC CONTRASTS PALETTE

White juxtaposed with a color tends to bleed, or weaken, the color contrast where the two colors meet. Black amplifies the color it is placed against. Gray is a chameleon, taking on the color characteristic of whatever it touches.

 Ivory

Bright White

 Ebony

 Gray Flannel

 Silver

Warm Gray

A pure palette of white swept on every surface gives this grand kitchen clean, sculptural lines.

Photo: Steve Vierra

Silver

Green Pear

Shiny, slick, and monochromatic, industrial kitchens like this one rely on food and accessories to add color and texture.

Photo: Tim Street-Porter

Gray Flint

Black Slate

Subtle values of gray make up this monochromatic color scheme. A skylight illuminates the monochromatic serenity of a black slate floor, aniline-dyed gray cabinetry, and polished granite.

Photo: Alan Weintraub

Photo: Tim Street-Porter

Bright White

Silver Gray

Poppy Red

A change from the obvious, color-flecked cabinets put a playful spin on the graphic style of this black and white kitchen.

Photo: Tim Street-Porter

Steel Gray

White Linen

Copper Wood

A galley kitchen receives sun through a skylight; a monochromatic scheme of pale tile, white painted beams and blond wood cabinetry also helps illuminate the narrow space.

Wine Red

Velvet

Stucco Gray

Photo: Donna Kempner

A simple combination of natural wood cabinetry and complementary blue walls opens out this airy kitchen alcove.

Gray Fleck

Grayed Green

Gray Sand

Tones and textures of white on white give this large cooking space a sophisticated atmosphere. Natural granite on the counter-tops draws warm color values out of the cabinetry. A subtle ribbon of checkerboard tile accentuates the white backsplash.

Photo: Laurie Black Photography

Velvet

Gray Moth

Gray Pewter

In kitchen design, materials can have as much impact as paint. Here, brushed stainless steel behaves like a light color against the dark polished surface of a natural stone countertop. Black makes the ceiling appear lower than it is, and guides the eye toward the french doors and cityscape beyond.

Photo: Rick Chapman

43

Photo: Steve Vierra

Black Slate

Bright White

Golden Citrus

Glass block in a pyramid window brings the horizon into this color scheme. The kitchen's cathedral ceiling arches high enough to carry off its citrus yellow color; while blue sky beyond the windows heightens the colorful impact.

Red Leather

Black Bird

Gray Birch

Accessories enliven the basic black and white palette of this angular kitchen; red counter stools offset the checkerboard floor.

Photo: Arch/Balthazar Korab

Photo: Kitchen by ALNO

Almond Wood

Neutral Gray

Metal Gray

This spacious kitchen uses value contrasts to create drama. Pale wood cabinetry is grounded by dark laminate counters. Neatly placed tile insets match the cabinets, becoming part of the palette.

Ghost

Stone Gray

Sleek finishes and high contrast colors of black and white dominate this kitchen. The complex curves of the island soften the overall atmosphere of the room.

Vanilla

Maplewood

Photo: Donna Kempner

Photo: Mark Darley/ESTO

For a softer contrast with the dark stainless steel fixtures, this design replaces traditional bright white with a vocabulary of white colors. The wood tones of a butcher block-island add warmth to the center of the room.

COLORS A LA CARTE
Dare-To-Be-Different Schemes

A La Carte colors create strong interiors and reflect confidence in your environment. "Color should be treated kindly, but it should never be allowed to get the best of the room."
—Elsie De Wolfe

Photo: Tim Street-Porter

Just like courses on a menu, colors can be put together in unexpected ways to give your kitchen the exact flavor you desire. The concept of a la carte colors is to dare to be different. Mix brilliant, sophisticated colors with the subtle tones of their complements . . . or do just the opposite. These schemes can be serious, or they can dance.

Accent colors spice up a kitchen palette. For example, even a small splash of yellow can balance a wide expanse of cool blue. Saturated colors like crimson, cobalt, and teal can convey a sense of visual energy.

 ● A LA CARTE PALETTE

Choose analogous or split complement colors from the color reference section of this book to create your own a la carte color schemes. Wood, stone, or concrete in shades a few steps lighter or darker than the main palette add texture and create interest.

 Crimson

 Pumpkin

 Cobalt

 Gold

 Teal

Cinnabar

Photo: "SEMANTICA" kitchen by Valcucine

High transom windows allow shafts of light to penetrate deeply into the room, illuminating teal cabinetry and the surprise of matching teal-finish appliances.

Heather

Cinnamon

Saffron

Buckskin

Iron Ore Red

Brass Gold

Crimson reinforces the geometry of this kitchen; outlining the diagonal motif of the granite back-splash, picking out the diamond shapes on the cabinetry, and emphasizing the pure rectangle of the oven. A copper hood embraces the room's natural warmth.

The warmth and boldness of red and yellow aniline-dyed wood, paired with cool blue and deep green tile, delivers colorful style.

Photo: Rick Chapman

Butter Cream

Spiced Pumpkin

Attention to detail lends interest to this simple kitchen. The black backsplash tiles are set on a diagonal, giving the surface added energy. Contrasts of value and color—white counter tile edged in black, and wood cabinetry against the black color—play an important role in the success of this kitchen.

Sunburst

Ecru

Bright yellow artic-ulates cabinetry, and gives a small kitchen spirit. This cheerful space illus-trates how the color of a room charges its atmosphere.

Photo: Kitchen by MIELE

Sea Spray

Butter Cream

Spice Red

Natural light from the french doors blends the golden tones of the cabinetry with the pale yellow wall color in this open kitchen. The pale green pantry door is unexpected, but makes a welcome bridge to the greenery visible outside. Ebony colored tile is a good foil for the antique Wedgewood stove.

Photo: Kitchen in ALNOPRO finish by ALNO

Natural Wood

Maple Syrup

Slate Blue

A triad color scheme of red-wood, pale yellow, and blue brings together contemporary cabinetry and traditional decor.

Pale Pumpkin

Golden Vanilla

*Pale orange lifts
a simple kitchen
into the realm of
the unexpected,
white ash cabinets
take on a peach
glow from the walls.*

Photo: Kitchen in ALNOLUX finish by ALNO

Photo: Tim Street-Porter

Berry

Radiant Gold

Foam Green

Berry colored plaster work softens the look of a shiny glass backsplash and upper cabinets in this kitchen.

Tourmaline Blue

Natural Wood

Photo: Kitchen in Alnoplan finish by ALNO

ROMANTIC TONES
Ethereal, Pale Palettes

Photo: Tim Street-Porter

Designing with the romantic palette creates rooms with *a light touch. These tinted kitchens reflect* *a calm, peaceful lifestyle. "Perfumes, colors, sounds echo* *one another."*
—Charles Baudelaire

P ale faded colors—reminiscent of hand-tinted photographs—create an ethereal, romantic kitchen color palette. Colors such as summer straw, lavender, peach, dried rose, herb green, and periwinkle blue have a soothing quality that is easy on the eye.

Often, red, yellow, and other strong warm shades are chosen for kitchens automatically because they are "traditional" kitchen colors. Light pastel tints create a different sort of atmosphere. Remember the scent of the beach after a storm, or recall the spectrum of green visible in a dense forest. These "color memories" can be a useful source of inspiration for creating a peaceful atmosphere in the kitchen.

Bleached oak gives this kitchen a soothing, alabaster cast. Green embellishes the "antique" quality of wicker chairs.

Photo: Kitchen by ALNO

 **● ROMANTIC TONES PALETTE**

Pure colors lightened by white are called pastels. When two or more colors are combined, and then intermixed with white, complex pastels are created. For example, the color lavender was created by adding a dash of red and black to blue, then adding white to the mixture. These fragile, subtle colors blend easily into complementary palettes of herb green and Venetian rose, in warm analogous combinations of summer straw and peach, or in cool analogous schemes of

 Summer Straw

 Lavender

 Peach

 Dried Rose

 Herb Green

Periwinkle Blue

Photo: Tim Street Porter

Venetian Rose

Spring Green

*Floral shades soften
the graphic power
of stripes in this
split-complement
scheme of Venetian
rose and green.*

Lambswool

Blonde Wood

Driftwood

Photo: Agnes Bourne

Green Leaf

Tendril Green

Rose Petal

*A wash of pale
rose softens the
appliances in
this tiny kitchen.
The clever shape
of a "petal" soffit
subtly extends
the floral theme.*

Photo: Tim Street-Porter

Soft color contrasts and diaphanous finishes make this grand kitchen graceful. Treating the floors, ceiling, walls, and cabinetry in close color values makes the space harmonious and soft.

Photo: Kitchen by Miele & Co. Ltd.

Warm Oak

Lapis Blue

Parchment

Rare blue marble gives this kitchen texture and color. The stone's fragile grain is an intriguing way to bring blue into the ivory and white palette.

Auburn

Baked Clay

Rustic pavers in
tints of peach and
straw-yellow link
this kitchen with
the rest of the house.

The warm rose of the tile floor keeps a blue color scheme from cooling the romance of this kitchen. Dresden blue on the ceiling, tiles, and embellishments pulls together the room's unusual shape.

Photo: Tim Street-Porter

Dresden Blue

Tuscan Red

Celestial blue pulled from the starry tile is used to pick out architectural detail and clever "utensil shelves" in an old-fashioned kitchen.

Photo: Tim Street Porter

Dutch Blue

Terra-Cotta

Glaze Blue

A surround of hand-painted tile focuses attention on the stove, the "heart" of the kitchen. Though brick and copper tones are abundant here—in the pans and in the floor tile—the predominance of white in the surround, cabinetry, and ceiling makes the atmosphere light.

65

Dried Herb

Fresh Herb

Peach Stone

Lichen Green

Apricot

A repeated ceiling arch and yellowed shades of orange and green bring together adjacent dining and living areas. Glazing on the walls lets white show through the paint, and keeps the shade subdued.

Herb green backsplash tile becomes a shelf and a window surround. Notice how using a range of green shades softens the effect of the tile.

COUNTRY PALETTE
Rich, Rustic Shades

Simplicity is the essence of country style. This style allows you to blend modern conve- *niences in a rustic, natural environment. "Only those who love color are admitted* *to its beauty and imminent presence. It affords utility to all, but unveils its* *deeper mysteries only to its devotees."*
—*Johannes Itten*

ountry style has a natural simplicity and practicality, taking its color cues from the land-scape and from regional building materials. The colors in this group are saturated and lively, like red pepper and majolica blue, or rich and complex, like baked clay and brown earth.

Use the humble materials of country decor to subdue the slick modernity of kitchen appliances and equipment. The natural textures and colors of wood, stone, brick, and tile will enhance your kitchen's rustic appeal.

● COUNTRY PALETTE

Since most natural materials have analogous warm colors, these shades are dominant in the country palette. Colors such as majolica blue and pine needle green can be introduced using paint or ceramic tile to balance the warm tones of terra-cotta floors and wood walls and cabinetry.

 Red Pepper

 Brown Earth

 Blue Bandanna

 Baked Clay

 Pine Needle Green

 Majolica Blue

Photo: Tim Street-Porter

Green leaves and a sanded green door-frame pull a bright yellow kitchen back to earth. A pool of bright blue tile on the countertop divides the cooking and eating areas of the room.

Hot Pepper

Evergreen

New Pine

*Seat cushions uphol-
stered in red pepper
hues add heat to a
pale white pine
kitchen. Saturated
colors make good
accents in rooms
dominated by a
lot of light wood.*

Photo: Steve Vierra

Cork

Rose Earth

Photo: Tim Street-Porter

Baked clay tile establishes a color rhythm in this open kitchen. Natural pine beams, and woven rush seats are a good combination with the worn texture of the floor.

Dedham Blue

Blue Haze

Bold blue hand-cut tiles add excitement to this space. The intensity of color in the tile draws attention away from the oversize double range.

Photo: Sam Gray Photography

Blue Tile

Glaze Red

Pale Stucco

Intricate patterns and tiles in saturated hues of blue, red, yellow and black give this kitchen the flavor of Mexico. Color combinations like this one can be used to create an exotic atmosphere.

Subtle color contrasts and diagonal patterns give this kitchen quiet energy. Complex shades of green on an ivory ground create an atmosphere of tranquility.

Sage Green

Chestnut

Grayed Green

The kitchen as theater: a graphic gray, green, and ivory painted wall makes a geometric backdrop for mismatched chairs, a rustic wooden door, and an oak dining table.

Photo: Daniel Clark

Ink Blue

Old Pine

The complementary colors of blue and orange are at work in this natural wood kitchen, lending visual interest to a collection of folk art. Country kitchens often rely on accessories for their colorful spark.

Photo: Arch/Balthazar Korab

Photo: Hedrich Blessing

Agate Green

Honey

*Texture creates color
and interest in this
neutral-toned space.
The juxtaposition
of smooth cabinets
and rough stone
emphasizes patterns
of light and shadow.*

Moss Stone

Brick Red

Tobacco Leaf

Photo: Arch/Balthazar Korab

Henna Brown

Old Brick

Tarragon

*Pale green shelves
complement the red
brick of a fireplace
wall. Chestnut and
golden brown tones
on the floor and ceil-
ing envelop the kitchen
with warmth.*

Photo: Mick Hales

Earth tones, rough-hewn beams, panelled walls, and mottled brick produce a rustic, cabin atmosphere. Contrasts in colors and materials are deliberately kept soft, to make the space feel restful.

Bold, Uncompromising Color

In the Urban Tech kitchen, color is never in a supporting role.

"Why do two colors put next to one another sing?"—Pablo Picasso.

Photo: "Latina" kitchen by Boffi, Milan, Italy

Attention-getting materials in strong colors are the foundation of Urban Tech's design freedom. Colors of strong chroma, such as acid green and mercury blue, make up this modern palette.

Stainless steel, aluminum, glass, laminates, and other industrial materials add muscle to the Urban Tech palette; since most of these surfaces have a glossy finish that intensifies color. The color schemes in this group run the gamut, from monochromatic to complementary, from analogous warm to cool, from split complementary to anything in-between. The defining element here is sleekness, whether it is bright red cabinets, or a shiny golden oak floor.

Man made and natural materials are boldly juxtaposed here, drawing the viewer into the space. Golden wood cabinetry contrasts with the concrete floor stained purple and ochre. Blue violet counters lit from above appear luminous.

● URBAN TECH
  PALETTE

Black is frequently used as an accent color in this dramatic palette; its graphic strength helps define and relate the other colors in the group.

 Acid Green

 Mercury Blue

 Chrome Yellow

 Siren Red

 Process Blue

 Black Steel

Photo: Walter Prina

Photo: Tim Street-Porter

Pecan

Red Copper

Quarry Stone

The subtle color contrast between the wall and wooden ceiling camouflages the change in planes, giving the room more height. An analogous color palette of red and orange radiates warmth.

Brushed Chrome

Blue Neon

Neon spikes a monochromatic gray scheme with color.

Photo: Kitchen by ALNO

Photo: Kitchen by ALNO

Vivid Green

Black Granite

Black granite polished to a mirror finish makes the floor seem to drop away in this kitchen design. The unusual contrast of bleached cabinetry with green walls is a refreshing combination.

Photo: Kitchen by ALNO

Glass Blue

Deep Blue

*Accents in glass blue
put some spark in
a domino-inspired
color scheme.*

Iron Gray

Blue Vapor

Pistachio Green

Photo: Kitchen by Miele

Photo: Kitchen by Miele

Spectra Yellow

Crystal Gray

The vibrant, stimulating quality of yellow cabinetry is tamed by pale gray tones on the vent, fixtures, and stovetop.

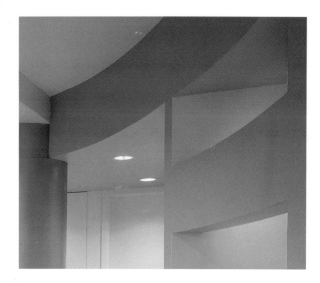

 Copper

 Sulphur

Color in this kitchen gives classic archi-tecture a modern twist with bright yellow sculpture alcoves and a copper-gilded column.

Photo: Paul Warchol

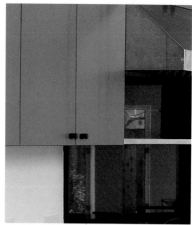

Washed Turquoise

Black Steel

Brushed Chrome

The curvaceous design of turquoise cabinetry stands out in bold relief against white walls. Although the color black usually absorbs light, here a highly polished black granite counter acts like a mirror—bringing natural light into the room.

Photo: Alan Weintraub

Scarlet

Blue Lake

Lemon Chrome

Methyl Blue

Four crayon-bright accent colors lend a playful air to a very modern kitchen. Notice the large scale European chrome hardware on the cabinetry.

Kitchen in "Merano" finish by Allmilmo

Sapphire

Yellow Pepper

Soapstone

Mercury Blue

Aluminum

Gray Metal

Mercury blue brings to life the heavy, industrial texture of a metal floor.

Blocks of deep blue dominate this small kitchen. Striped patterns of black and white on the floor provide visual stimulation. The clever use of black laminate on the kitchen island draws the eye upward.

Photo: "Contemporanea" Kitchen by Snaidero R.S.P.A., Milano, Italy

Straw

Flint Steel

Redwood

Matte black countertops and the black triangular wedge of a stove hood combine successfully with the low shine of a brushed stainless steel sink and matching appliances. This kitchen has modern style, but the warm wood of the cabinetry keeps it from being clinical and cold.

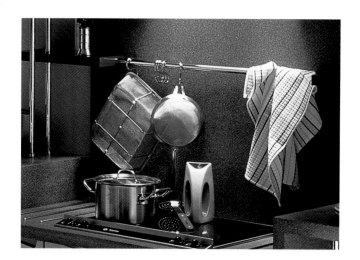

 Primary Blue

 Primary Red

Primary Yellow

Wedges of primary color are working cabinet pulls that bring strong color to the space in a surprising way.

ECO-COLORS
Earthy, Natural Combinations

Photo: Geoffrey Gross

Eco-colors are elemental. Taking their cues from the natural environment, the copper, green, and red shades of this palette can set kitchen designs ablaze with color. "Color is a sort of food; every spot of color is a drop of wine to the heart."
—*Richard Jefferie*

Lava Red

 Copper

 Tundra Taupe

 Evergreen

 Olive

 Chestnut Brown

The eco-color palette takes its inspiration from natural elements: earth, air, fire, and water. Renewed interest in the environment has spurred an interest in organic colors as well. When used in the kitchen these colors may be strong and saturated, but their natural tones give them a subdued, earthy appeal.

Texture plays an important role in the eco-color story. Materials, rather than paint, often dictate eco-color schemes. Wood, stone, and metals have strong color presence, and bring the natural environment to your kitchen interior.

These colors are created by intermixing two or more colors. For example, to achieve an olive shade you would mix green with small proportions of red and yellow, then add a touch of black to shade the color. Complex colors have a great deal of depth and richness and may be combined into complementary, analogous warm, or cool color schemes.

Color plays a low-key role in this natural wood kitchen. Bright blue painted window frames and accessories add to the kitchen's country charm.

Photo: Doug Keister Photography

Photo: David Livingston

Bayberry

Mahogany

*Designed to blend harmoniously
with Arts and Crafts-style decor,
this kitchen's palette was intentionally
kept rich and dark. The dark values
of black and green on the countertop
and backsplash are balanced by a
wash of golden color on the walls,
and mahogany stained lower cabinets.*

94

Lily Green

Walnut Brown

Pale Taupe

Scale plays an important role in this elegant kitchen as the cool green and ivory color scheme works to expand the room.

Photo: Alan Weintraub

Photo: Linda Svendsen

Warm Taupe

Sagebrush

Evergreen

Natural tones of taupe call attention to the ruddy tones of a sleek kitchen-island.

Chestnut Brown

Pale Olive

Stone Gray

The shine of copper pots and pans compliments this kitchen's grayed down palette. Grey veining in the white marble countertop echoes the grey tones in the green walls, and contrasts with chestnut stained cabinets.

Photo: Mick Hales

Golden Taupe

Forest Green

Enamel Red

A delicate mix of marble diamond shapes and inlaid brass brings a cornucopia of visual stimulation to light wood surfaces.

Photo: John Vaughan

Copper Leaf

Green Pepper

Coffee Bean

Faux-painted copper walls radiate with intensity. The high contrast of color on the ceiling draws attention to exposed beams. Crisp white cabinetry and open shelving set the stage for a colorful display of Mexican folk art.

Granite

Polished Brown

Fieldstone

A stone floor and counters, mahogany cabinets and marble tile give this formal kitchen elemental appeal.

Photo: Steve Vierra

Photo: Steve Vierra

Granite

Clove Brown

Kilim Red

Cabinets dyed burnt sienna blend easily with a polished granite countertop and backsplash. The gray tones of faux-finished walls add even more depth to the saturated colors of the kitchen.

Photo: David Livingston

Photo: E. Andrew McKinney

Photo: Rick Clingerman

Cherry Red

Golden Oak

Olive Gray

Shale Green

Antique Brick

Berry Stain

A simple scheme of red and green complementary colors frames the view and defines the cabinetry. The white rectangular tiles used on the counter and backsplash are typical of a late 19th century kitchen.

The light value of gray and white marble sets off redwood cabinetry. Though this kitchen appears very colorful, notice that its palette is entirely natural materials—no paint is used in the room.

Desert

Volcano Red

Blue Spruce

A gemologist selected the innovative hammered stainless steel and lustrous tile finishes used in this kitchen. The volcanic red glaze on the backsplash looks as if it's on fire—heightening the drama of the room.

Photo: Elliot Kaufman

Watercress Green

Adobe Brown

Butcher Block

An unusual mix of elements marries old and new. Saturated green cabinets highlight plain wood countertops and smooth terra-cotta floor tile. An antique wrought iron light fixture overlooks the modern rectangle of a stainless steel range and hood.

COLOR
SWATCHES

BRAVE NEW COLORS
Strong and Energetic Color Schemes

TINTS

SHADES

Main Palette	Tints	Shades
Riviera Blue	Tinted Riviera Blue	Shaded Riviera Blue
Chanel Red	Tinted Chanel Red	Shaded Chanel Red
Ivy Green	Tinted Ivy Green	Shaded Ivy Green
Daffodil Yellow	Tinted Daffodil Yellow	Shaded Daffodil Yellow
Mandarin Orange	Tinted Mandarin Orange	Shaded Mandarin Orange
Iris Purple	Tinted Iris Purple	Shaded Iris Purple

Chapter 2 — Main Palette
ECLECTIC CONTRASTS
Crisp, Sophisticated Shades

ECLECTIC CONTRASTS	TINTS	SHADES
Bright White		
Ivory	Tinted Ivory	Shaded Ivory
Ebony	Tinted Ebony	
Gray Flannel	Tinted Gray Flannel	Shaded Gray Flannel
Silver	Tinted Silver	Shaded Silver
Warm Gray	Tinted Warm Gray	Shaded Warm Gray

Chapter 3 — Main Palette COLORS A LA CARTE *Dare-To-Be-Different Schemes*	TINTS	SHADES
Crimson	Tinted Crimson	Shaded Crimson
Pumpkin	Tinted Pumpkin	Shaded Pumpkin
Cobalt	Tinted Cobalt	Shaded Cobalt
Gold	Tinted Gold	Shaded Gold
Teal	Tinted Teal	Shaded Teal
Cinnabar	Tinted Cinnabar	Shaded Cinnabar

Chapter 4 — Main Palette ROMANTIC TONES *Ethereal, Pale Palettes*		TINTS		SHADES	
	Summer Straw		Tinted Summer Straw		Shaded Summer Straw
	Lavender		Tinted Lavender		Shaded Lavender
	Peach		Tinted Peach		Shaded Peach
	Dried Rose		Tinted Dried Rose		Shaded Dried Rose
	Herb Green		Tinted Herb Green		Shaded Herb Green
	Periwinkle Blue		Tinted Periwinkle Blue		Shaded Periwinkle Blue

Chapter 5 — Main Palette COUNTRY PALETTE *Rich, Rustic Shades*		TINTS		SHADES	
	Red Pepper		Tinted Red Pepper		Shaded Red Pepper
	Brown Earth		Tinted Brown Earth		Shaded Brown Earth
	Blue Bandanna		Tinted Blue Bandanna		Shaded Blue Bandanna
	Baked Clay		Tinted Baked Clay		Shaded Baked Clay
	Pine Needle Green		Tinted Pine Needle Green		Shaded Pine Needle Green
	Majolica Blue		Tinted Majolica Blue		Shaded Majolica Blue

URBAN TECH
Bold, Uncompromising Colors

TINTS

SHADES

URBAN TECH	TINTS	SHADES
Acid Green	Tinted Acid Green	Shaded Acid Green
Mercury Blue	Tinted Mercury Blue	Shaded Mercury Blue
Chrome Yellow	Tinted Chrome Yellow	Shaded Chrome Yellow
Siren Red	Tinted Siren Red	Shaded Siren Red
Process Blue	Tinted Process Blue	Shaded Process Blue
Black Steel	Tinted Black Steel	

Chapter 7 — Main Palette
ECO-COLORS
Earthy, Natural Combinations

ECO-COLORS	TINTS	SHADES
Lava Red	Tinted Lava Red	Shaded Lava Red
Copper	Tinted Copper	Shaded Copper
Tundra Taupe	Tinted Tundra Taupe	Shaded Tundra Taupe
Evergreen	Tinted Evergreen	Shaded Evergreen
Olive	Tinted Olive	Shaded Olive
Chestnut Brown	Tinted Chestnut Brown	Shaded Chestnut Brown

Cornsilk Yellow Page 24	Cobalt Page 26	Cornhusk Yellow Page 28
Red Ember Page 24	Wheat Page 26	Lilac Page 28
Sunset Orange Page 24	True Red Page 27	Bright Red Page 30
Topaz Page 25	Chrome Yellow Page 28	Spinach Green Page 30
Gray Sand Page 25	Carnelian Page 28	Canary Yellow Page 30
Pompeii Red Page 25	Vineyard Green Page 28	Sage Green Page 30
Red Geranium Page 26	Herb Green Page 28	Golden Glow Page 30

	Ochre Page 30		Celery Green Page 32		Kumquat Orange Page 35
	Garnet Page 31		Olive Gray Page 32		Green Pear Page 38
	Fern Green Page 31		Grenadine Orange Page 34		Gray Flint Page 38
	Oriental Blue Page 31		Fawn Page 34		Black Slate Page 38, 44
	Shell Coral Page 32		Shadow Blue Page 34		Silver Grey Page 39
	Gray Dawn Page 32		Blue Lake Page 35		Poppy Red Page 39
	Citrus Yellow Page 32		Rouge Page 35		Steel Gray Page 40

White Linen Page 40	Gray Sand Page 42	Almond Wood Page 46
Copper Wood Page 40	Gray Moth Page 43	Neutral Gray Page 46
Wine Red Page 40	Gray Pewter Page 43	Metal Gray Page 46
Velvet Page 40, 43	Golden Citrus Page 44	Ghost Page 46
Stucco Gray Page 40	Red Leather Page 45	Stone Gray Page 46
Gray Fleck Page 42	Black Bird Page 45	Vanilla Page 46
Grayed Green Page 42, 74	Gray Birch Page 45	Maplewood Page 46

Buckskin Page 50	Spiced Pumpkin Page 52	Slate Blue Page 54
Iron Ore Red Page 50	Sunburst Page 52	Pale Pumpkin Page 55
Brass Gold Page 50	Ecru Page 52	Golden Vanilla Page 55
Heather Page 50	Sea Spray Page 53	Berry Page 56
Cinnamon Page 50	Spice Red Page 53	Radiant Gold Page 56
Saffron Page 50	Natural Wood Page 54, 56	Foam Green Page 56
Butter Cream Page 50, 53	Maple Syrup Page 54	Tourmaline Blue Page 56

	Venetian Rose		Driftwood		Tuscan Red
	Page 60		Page 60		Page 64
	Spring Green		Warm Oak		Dutch Blue
	Page 60		Page 62		Page 65
	Green Leaf		Lapis Blue		Terra-Cotta
	Page 60		Page 62		Page 65
	Tendril Green		Parchment		Glaze Blue
	Page 60		Page 62		Page 65
	Rose Petal		Auburn		Lichen Green
	Page 60		Page 63		Page 66
	Lambswool		Baked Clay		Apricot
	Page 60		Page 63		Page 66
	Blonde Wood		Dresden Blue		Dried Herb
	Page 60		Page 64		Page 66

	Fresh Herb Page 66		Dedham Blue Page 70		Ink Blue Page 75
	Peach Stone Page 66		Blue Haze Page 72		Old Pine Page 75
	Hot Pepper Page 70		Blue Tile Page 73		Agate Green Page 76
	Evergreen Page 70		Glaze Red Page 73		Honey Page 76
	New Pine Page 70		Pale Stucco Page 73		Henna Brown Page 76
	Cork Page 70		Chestnut Page 74		Old Brick Page 76
	Rose Earth Page 70		Sage Green Page 74		Tarragon Page 76

Moss Stone Page 76	Quarry Stone Page 80	Pistachio Green Page 82
Brick Red Page 76	Vivid Green Page 81	Spectra Yellow Page 84
Tobacco Leaf Page 76	Black Granite Page 81	Crystal Gray Page 84
Brushed Chrome Page 80	Glass Blue Page 82	Copper Page 85
Blue Neon Page 80	Deep Blue Page 82	Sulphur Page 85
Pecan Page 80	Iron Gray Page 82	Washed Turquoise Page 86
Red Copper Page 80	Blue Vapor Page 82	Black Steel Page 86

Scarlet Page 87	Sapphire Page 88	Primary Red Page 91
Blue Lake Page 87	Yellow Pepper Page 88	Primary Yellow Page 91
Lemon Chrome Page 87	Soapstone Page 88	Bayberry Page 94
Methyl Blue Page 87	Straw Page 90	Mahogany Page 94
Mercury Blue Page 88	Flint Steel Page 90	Lily Green Page 95
Aluminum Page 88	Redwood Page 90	Chestnut Brown Page 95, 96
Gray Metal Page 88	Primary Blue Page 91	Pale Taupe Page 95

	Pale Olive
Page 96		Enamel Red
Page 98		Clove Brown
Page 100
	Stone Gray
Page 96		Copper Leaf
Page 98		Kilim Red
Page 100
	Warm Taupe
Page 97		Green
Pepper
Page 98		Shale Green
Page 102
	Sagebrush
Page 97		Coffee Bean
Page 98		Antique Brick
Page 102
	Evergreen
Page 97		Granite
Page 100		Berry Stain
Page 102
	Golden
Taupe
Page 98		Polished
Brown
Page 100		Cherry Red
Page 102
	Forest Green
Page 98		Fieldstone
Page 100		Golden Oak
Page 102

Olive Gray Page 102	
Desert Page 104	
Volcano Red Page 104	
Blue Spruce Page 104	
Watercress Green Page 105	
Adobe Brown Page 105	
Butcher Block Page 105	

COLOR GLOSSARY

Analogous Color Scheme — A scheme that uses three colors (or their tints and shades) that are next to each other on the color wheel.

Chroma — Chroma is the degree of brilliance of a color.

Complementary Color Scheme — A color scheme that uses colors from opposite sides of the color wheel.

Hue — Hue is the formal term for color.

Monochromatic Color Scheme — A color scheme that uses only variations of one color, or a scheme that uses only white, black, and gray.

Saturation — Saturation is the intensity or brightness of a color.

Shades — Shades (or dark values) are colors with black added to them.

Split Complementary Scheme — A color scheme made up of any color combined with two colors on either side of its complement on the color wheel.

Temperature — The perceived warmth or coolness of a color.

Tints — Tints (or light tonal values) are colors with white added to them.

Triad Color Scheme — A color scheme that uses three colors (or their tints or shades) that are equidistant on the color wheel.

Value — Value (or tonal value) is the relative lightness or darkness of a color.

Our special thanks to those photographers, architects, and designers who graciously contributed their work to make this book a reality.

PHOTOGRAPHERS

Allmilmö Corporation

Alno Corporation

Arc linea

Arch/Balthazar Korab Ltd.

Richard Barnes, Photographer

Laurie Black

Boffi Spa

Rick Chapman, Photographer

Daniel Clark Photography

Rik Clingerman

Philip Cohen

© Mark Darley/Esto

Sam Gray Photography

Geoffrey Gross

Mick Hales

Hedrick-Blessing

Elliot Kaufman

Douglas Keister Photography

Donna Kempner Architectural Photography

David Livingston

E. Andrew McKinney

Miele & Co., Ltd

Mark Sinclair Architectural Photography

Smallbone Cabinetry

Snaidero R. Spa

Strato

Tim Street-Porter

Linda Svendsen Photography

Val Cucine

John Vaughan Photography

Steve Vierra

Paul Warchol

Alan Weintraub

ARCHITECTS/DESIGNERS

Ace Architects

Architects II

Bauer Interior Design

Kutnicki/Bernstein Architects

Barbara Berry

Agnes Bourne, Inc.

Laura Guido Clark/Beverly Thome Design

Craig Franklin

David Hale, Architect

Jerrit Hedbor

Hodgetts & Fung

House + House

Holly Hulburd

Hutton & Wilkinson

Erik Kramvik Design: cabinets designed by William Eichenberger

Francisco Kripacz

Piero Lissoni

Mark Mack

Manolo Mestre

Brian Murphy

Noble/Simon

Robert Noble

Osburn Design

Charles Riley

Richard Rouilard

Steve Rynerson

John Schlenke, AIA

Freya Serabian

Peter Shire

Stamberg Aferiat Architecture

Cindy Sterry

Stiles and Clements, Architects

Bruce Tomb/John Randolph

BIBLIOGRAPHY

Ackerman, Diane. *A Natural History of the Senses*. New York: Vintage Books, 1990.

Alexander, Christopher. *A Pattern Language*. New York: Oxford University Press, 1977.

Birren, Faber. *Color Psychology and Color Therapy*. Secaucus, NJ: University Books, 1961.

Birren, Faber. *Color - A Survey in Words and Pictures*. Secaucus, NJ: Citadel Press, 1963.

Birren, Faber. *Light, Color & Environment*. Westchester, NY: Schiffer Publishing Ltd., 1988.

Bustanoby, J.H. *Principles of Color and Color Mixing*. New York: McGraw Hill, 1947.

Calloway, Stephen, and Elizabeth Cromley. *Elements of Style*. New York: Simon & Schuster, 1991.

Conran, Terence. *Kitchen Book*. Woodstock, NY: Overlook Press, 1993.

Guild, Tricia. *Tricia Guild On Color*. New York: Rizzoli, 1993.

Hope, Augustine, and Margaret Walch. *The Color Compendium*. New York: Van Nostrand Reinhold, 1990.

Itten, Johannes. *Itten: The Elements of Color*. New York: Van Nostrand Reinhold, 1970.

Leland, Nita. *Exploring Color*. Cincinnati, OH: North Light Books, 1985.

Madden, Chris Casson. *Kitchens*. New York: Clarkson N. Potter, Inc., 1993.

Mahnke, Frank H. and Rudolph H. Mahnke. *Color and Light in Man-Made Environments*. New York: Van Nostrand Reinhold, 1987.

Sidelinger, Stephen J. *Color Manual*. Englewood Cliffs, NJ: Prentice Hall, 1985.

Sloane, Patricia. *Primary Sources*. New York: Design Press, 1991.

Swirnoff, Lois. *Dimensional Color*. Boston: Birkhauser Boston, Inc., 1988.

DIRECTORY OF KITCHEN
SUPPLIERS & MANUFACTURERS

Abbaka
435 23rd Street
San Francisco, CA 94107

Aga Cookers Inc.
17 Town Farm Lane
Stowe, VT 05672

Aga Rayburn
P.O. Box 30
Ketley Telford
Shropshire
TFI 4DD
England

Allmilmö Corp.
P.O. Box 629
70 Clinton Road
Fairfield, NJ 07004-2976

Mileweski Mobelwerk
Obere Altach #1
97475 ZEIL AM MAIN
Germany

Alno Network USA
1 Design Center Place #643
Boston, MA 02210

Amana Refrigeration
Amana, IA 52204

American Olean Tile Co.
1000 Cannon Avenue
Lansdale, PA 19446

American Standard Inc.
1 Centennial Plaza
P.O. Box 6820
Piscataway, NJ 08855

Boffi Arredamento Cucina, SPA
Via G Oberdan
20030 Lentate Sul Seveso
Milan
Italy

Corian Products
DuPont Co.
PPD Dept.
Wilmington, DE 19898

Eljer Industries
901 10th street
Plano, TX 75074

Formica Corporation
10155 Reading Road
Cincinnati, OH 45241

Franke
Kitchen Systems Division
212 Church Road
North Wales, PA 19454-4140

Franke AG
CH-4663 Aaburg
Switzerland

Gaggenau
425 University Avenue
Norwood, MA 02062

Gaggenau Werke
Eisenwerkstr. 11
76571 Gaggenau
Germany

General Electric
GE Appliances
Appliance Park
Louisville, KY 40225

George Kovacs Lighting, Inc.
67-25 Otto Road
Glendale, NY 11385

Groen
1900 Pratt Boulevard
Elk Grove Village, IL 60007

Grohe
900 Lively Boulevard
Wood Dale, Il 60191

Hastings Tile — Il Bagno Collection
30 Commercial Street
Freeport, NY 11520

Italian Tile Center
The Italian Trade Commission
499 Park Avenue
New York, NY 10022

Italian Trade Commission
via Liszt-21
00144 Rome
Italy

JADO Bath & Hardware Mfg. Co.
P.O. Box 1329
1690 Calle Quetzal
Camarillo, CA 93011

Jenn-Air
3035 Shadeland
Indianapolis, IN 46226

Kitchen Aid
701 Main Street
St. Joseph, MI 49085

Kohler Co.
Kohler, WI 53044

Lightolier Inc.
100 Lighting Way
Secaucus, NJ 07096

Miele & Cie.
GmbH & Co.
Carl-Miele-Strasse 29
D-33332 Gutersloh

Poggenpol, U.S., Inc.
5905 Johns Road
Tampa, FL 33634

Porcher
3618 East LaSalle
Phoenix, AZ 85040

SieMatic
886 Town Center Drive
Langhorne, PA 19047

SieMatic Mobelwerk
GmbH and Co.
August- Siekmann-
Strasse
D-32584 Lohne
Germany

Smallbone, Inc.
886 Town Center Drive
Langhorne, PA 19047

Snaidero International USA
201 West 132 Street
Los Angeles, CA 90061

Snaidero R. SPA
via Europa Unita 9
33030 Majano (UP)
Italy

Strato
Sedevia Piemonte 9
23018
Talamona (SD)
Italy

Swedish Rehab-Division of Lumex
100 Spence Street
Bay Shore, NY 11706

Traulsen & Co., Inc.
114-02 15th Avenue
College Point, NY 11356

Val Cucine
Via Maglignani, 5
33170 Pordenone
Italy

Viking Range Corp.
111 Front Street
Greenwood, MS 38930

Waterford Irish Stoves Inc.
16 Air Park Road #3
West Lebanon, NH 03784-9701

Waterford Stanley
Bilberry
Waterford City
Country Waterford
Ireland

들 • Le Cucine • מטבח • Cozinhas • Kit

Les cuisines • 廚房 • Mutfaklar • 부엌들 • Le

chen • Keukens • ห้องครัวหลายห้อง • Les cui

ozinhas • Kitchens • 台所 • Las Cocinas • K

房 • Mutfaklar • 부엌들 • Le Cucine • מטבח

eukens • ห้องครัวหลายห้อง • Les cuisines • 廚

tchens • 台所 • Las Cocinas • Küchen • Keuk

부엌들 • Le Cucine • מטבח • Cozinhas • Kitc

s cuisines • 廚房 • Mutfaklar • 부엌들 • Le C

üchen • Keukens • ห้องครัวหลายห้อง • Les cu

zinhas • Kitchens • 台所 • Las Cocinas • Kü

Mutfaklar • 부엌들 • Le Cucine • מטבח • Coz

งครัวหลายห้อง • Les cuisines • 廚房 • Mutfak

所 • Las Cocinas • Küchen • Keukens • ห้อ

Cucine • מטבח • Cozinhas • Kitchens • 台所